*Advice to a Young Wife
from an Old Mistress*

By Michael Drury

Advice to a Young Wife from an Old Mistress

as told to
MICHAEL DRURY

Four Directions
Press

Published by Four Directions Press, 88 Astor Square,
P. O. Box 417, Rhinebeck, New York 12572

International Standard Book Number 0-9627659-5-3
Library of Congress Catalog Card Number 93-72452

Manufactured in the United States of America

Book design by Sean J. McCarthy & Sally Keil

Second Edition

To Margaret Cousins,

editor *extraordinaire*, teacher, friend.

ACKNOWLEDGEMENT

When I met the woman I have here written about, it was as though I had met myself (for I, too am a woman, despite my errant name); a self I had imagined, tasted, searched for, by turns coaxed and dismissed as irrational in the twentieth century. I knew only that she was brave, as I should like to have been and be; that she knew something at once secret and open; that she was immensely real. I asked, a little clumsily, if I might interview her, about what I did not quite know. This was a woman I felt compelled to hear. She was willing, but wary. We left the social gathering where our paths had crossed, and she took me to her home. In her living room were five renowned paintings that staggered me—eye, mind, and heart. For several minutes I studied them in silence, all eagerness to talk forgotten. When at last I turned and sat down on a sofa, it was as if I had been slammed onto it by an unseen hand. Perceiving this, she smiled—and the book was begun.

It was much later that I understood why.

Contents

The Vital Factor

I n Spanish one answers the telephone by saying, not hello, but, on formal occasions, "With whom do I speak?" That may sound peremptory in English, but on a soft Iberian tongue it has an Old World courtesy and music. It is the way I think of you, whoever you are. I wonder about you and I salute you. With whom do I speak? Are you my own earlier, younger self, and would I have listened then, or understood? A young wife—I have not forgotten—is in a super-sentient mood, an attentive state that can hear perhaps more acutely than at any other time in her life, except possibly just after the birth of a child.

I remember because, for all my seventy-four years, I am more like you than you might suppose. A mistress shares a secret with a newly wedded wife: that love is a kind of glorious grief, equidistant from happiness and tears. In twenty years the bond between us shall have dissolved, unless I speak. Of course I should no longer be here, but I mean dissolution of another sort, a coming to nothing of what now fills your life with promise to the brim; the everyday stalemate so commonplace no one takes it very seriously, except young wives and mistresses.

I am apt to be more like you than your mother, who long ago determined the shape all love must take, and has forgotten that each day's choices, even now, have anything to do with it. Nor is she wholly wrong. Love lived from day to day takes on a momentum of its own, but that is not the all of it. If a mistress knows more of romance and a wife more of practicalities, is there not some wholeness implied here worthwhile to explore?

It is not my intention to set wives against mistresses more than is inherent in their situation, or to try to prove one better than the other. Rather, I would show that they have much in common as women—and womanness comes first for all of us. To learn that is the basis of living and loving well. In time, if they are wise enough, wives and mistresses can learn from one another as from no one else. In time: I write from a long road of years—years of living and dying a little; of humbling and exalta-

14

tion; of slow coming to know myself and thus other people more completely. That is one advantage a mistress has, simply as a human being, over a wife: she is in the nature of things more exposed to the contrary currents of living. She must master them, or perish; grow all the way up to whatever powers she was born with and ride them as a man rides a surfboard standing up, or drown. She is made to be a realist; that is to say, to realize herself. It is one of the richest blessings life can bestow.

But one does not know that in the beginning, and it is not why I became a mistress. I could almost write this the other way around, if I chose. Mistresses have to learn like anybody else from observation and mistakes, and it is often wives who prove the ablest teachers, both by what they do and fail of doing—or of seeing. I know, for I too was once a wife, and in love, and in earnest—and suddenly was faced with the fact of another woman in my husband's life. I had been married quite a while and was the mother of one son. What followed was divorce, against my wishes it seemed at first, although the marriage was a shell and I soon realized its termination was the more honorable outcome, and was at peace.

I had longed with all my heart for an important and enduring love, but that was finished now. I could not go back to being twenty, and one gets past naïve believing. But the spirit has a deeper knowledge, so translucent that one may not know it exists until some slant of light or storm reveals it. Be careful of what you want; it has a way of turning up when and where one least expects it. Be sure you are strong enough to live with it when it happens.

In two years' time I met a man who was at once a walking image taken from my mind and almost aloof in his self-possession. We met by the accident of our work, which, though not the same, over-lapped. I was waiting for him in an office—his—lined with five famous paintings of museum quality. I had seen many prints of them but never the originals, and I was looking at one when he came in. The first words I ever spoke to him were, "How do you stand it?" and he replied, "How would I stand it without them?"

From that moment we began a friendship rich in undertones but without complications or con-straint. I thought of him as evidence of the human potential, and a little as a model for myself, but, as a foreign friend of mine says with finality, "no else." I knew he was married and, for reasons not mine to disclose, would never of his own accord undo it. He told me that, but in a context so remote from myself that when he first suggested a deeper relationship for us, I was wholly astonished. It was some weeks before the issue was resolved, but I knew in less than a day that it was out there waiting for us, almost written, as the Arabs say. Almost, but not quite, for I do not believe people are that helpless. Certainly we were not. We had a choice and made it. The strongest thing I felt was recognition, as if I had known this man very long ago. Somewhere Montaigne says, "We sought each other long before we met... We found ourselves so mutually taken with one another, so acquainted and so endeared betwixt ourselves, that from thence forward nothing was ever so near to us as one another... Being begun so late, there was no time to lose."

You may say that what I did was selfish and that, I think, is true, but not in the way that word is commonly construed. Very little of any moment happens until self-interest is aroused—no wealth or power or art or faith or government; what men and nations desire rules the world. Right and wrong are absolutes, and human beings seldom have the luxury of absolute choice between them. Given the forces that were released simply by our encounter—and that much was not our doing— was it more or less brave to yield to them along with their concomitants of taste, restraint, the abrasion of disapproval from ourselves and others? Was it more or less gallant to break the rules or to walk away from a gift "far above rubies"? There can be no starkly correct answers; that is the truth one finds at first terribly difficult, so ingrained are the inherited expectations of a copybook standard. One thing I learned was that human beings make decisions as wisely as they can, and then make them right or wrong by the terms on which they live with those decisions.

I had four dominant emotions that I can state—there were others, of course, but I do not propose to talk of that. For the first time in my life, I took my own destiny into my own hands. Whatever happened, there was no place to run to; for good or ill, it would have to be borne alone. Until one claims the native right of going out on one's own irreparable limb, full-scale maturity is not attained, no matter how well one functions in other respects.

Secondly, I was a friend to all the universe. I felt myself linked to a great chain of human beings, known and unknown, past and present. I got a strangely comprehensive sense of history, as if I were seeing it and myself right side up and in perspective, neither of world-shattering importance nor of cosmic insignificance.

Third, I tasted power in becoming. Some qualities were at last tempered without struggle, like possessiveness and a shade too much intensity; others were added or increased: serenity, humor, a decent fatalism. I felt almost put to school in a course I had signed up for long ago but had not found the place where it was held.

And underlying it all was a pervading surprise at not being engulfed by shame. Far from it: I felt three-dimensional, whole, alive. I was not unmindful of my wrong position, and I had no defense for it. One does not apologize for self-discovery.

I shall call him Matthew, for to speak of him at all without clumsiness or sham, I must call him something. The word *lover*, applied to a specific person, has always seemed to me distasteful. It is at once too poetical and too graphic, and I find both repugnant. I expect I am old-fashioned in some ways. To call him merely my friend, although he was, slurs the extraordinary quality of that friendship by leaving out so much else.

It may seem curious that among the lessons of an illicit love is a discreet use of words, but it is, and this precision in turn enhances the relationship and in some measure explains the reason for it. The longing not to be nothing is one of the sharpest hungers a human being can know. Men in prison

19

have rioted for names instead of numbers. To address another person by his name is a significant way of affirming his identity, of registering it. Words are not merely dead things, and especially names are not; they partly create the substance they denominate. Word and idea, name and identity, attract one another. Words are alive; they move, they bend, evoke, bear witness to the inner state of him who speaks. A woman can scatter *darling* so heedlessly that its meaning is first diluted, then doubted, then quite dead. A man deserves better than *darling*, any of several on the block, and to speak to a man directly and exclusively as *daddy* is outrageous. He is not the wife's daddy and calling him so is a public announcement that she had lost all track of him as a person; he is somebody after all, Peter or Tom or Bill. A mistress learns the power and significance of a name instead of a sobriquet.

Matthew fits the style of his real name, and both fit the style of the man: straightforward, male, dignified without stuffiness, a no-nonsense name. He could laugh, but basically he thought life serious; to believe otherwise was cheap.

I have said I am old-fashioned, and it gratifies my late-Victorian upbringing to think that that is so. It also, I admit, amuses my later twentieth-century sense of comic justice. I find it funny that I,

who for almost thirty years was mistress to an
eminent man and no little scandal, should now be
the outraged and proper one, upholder of the old
order. Funny and yet sad, for what shocks me is the
dehumanization of love by young and wholly legal
wives who chop and nail down and reduce that
powerful force to a technique no different from
driving a car or mastering the methods of good
grooming. I am appalled by their consumer approach, their concern with management, their inef-
fectuality as women—sexless, competitive,
anxiety-ridden. Can they honestly mistake such
programming for the spirit that unifies their own
pulses with the great rhythms of the universe? Do
they truly believe that experts with no source of
information except what is said by others—since a
felt experience can only be perceived within—can
tell them more about their feelings than those feelings can?

What has become of joy, and sorrow? I, who
broke hearts including at times my own, am horrified by cool-eyed young women scientifically certain that a heart cannot possibly break. It is an
organ, like a liver, nothing more; and they can
prove it. The proof is unarguable, and serenely
fraudulent. I, who defied the world and ultimately
made a truce with it, certainly never invited it into

my bedroom. Have women no instincts any more, no mystery or mettle? Must everything be subjected to instruction and manuals, as if love were a kind of cooking school?

I am not so old-fashioned that I do not know the current cult: if total physical rapture is lacking, the mechanism needs tuning up, and the wise couple seeks professional help. The very concept is self-defeating and simply wrong. The more conscious they become of what "ought" to be the case, the farther they are removed from the spontaneity, skill, surprise, and delight they desire, and the whole thing compounds itself. Whoever heard of lovers reading up on procedure? Can you imagine Romeo and Juliet consulting some Elizabethan research report to find out if they fit the norm?

If a marriage can be rescued by such tinkering, I myself have never known of one that was. By creating the appearance of something actually going on, it may postpone the inevitable collapse, but genuine relation cannot be concocted, even with the greatest good will in the world. Only married people would try: lovers simply part. This is another boon a mistress has: she is human and can fool herself, but not for long. Nothing in society or in the situation encourages her in the pretext of a love that doesn't exist. Thus a certain honesty and sanity invite her company. She has or soon acquires a candor that is as enticing as cold mountain air after the stuffy rooms of fantasy and fear.

Martin Buber, the Israeli philosopher who was greatly occupied with all kinds of human encounter, had no patience with any erotic concepts measured by mere enjoyment, no matter how mutual or glorious. He insisted upon whole self as the key ingredient, and said, "He who would give new life to marriage from another source is not essentially different from him who would abolish it. Both clearly show that they no longer know the vital factor." He wrote that in 1923. When I came across it many years later, I felt as though he had written it for me, as of course he had. He wrote it for anyone who lives into existence enough of his vital factor to know what he meant—and by that time I had done so.

I would put it this way: What really matters is not marriage but relatedness. Marriage is indispensable for the common good, but it does not by itself constitute pure relation, and we forget its subsidiary position to our peril. A mistress cares nothing for theories and norms, "how men are" as a species or "what a woman needs", any woman, abstract woman. She is immediately and intensely caught up in one man, as original as Adam, and in her own experience with him, and this can be felt like a magnetic field. If her cast of temperament concurs with that of other women, that is neither for it nor against it. If what exists between her and the man is unprecedented or as old as time, neither fact either justifies or condemns the romance.

Because a mistress is outside society to begin with, she is less subject to its pressures, which in our day are mainly mechanistic: cause and effect, classification, probability. When a man is pleased with her, it is in defiance of explanations. If he is angry, it is for his own reasons, just or unjust, and not because men subconsciously resent women or are frustrated by an industrialized society. He is with her almost as when he is alone, singular man, sovereign as man was meant to be, not over the woman nor even himself so much as over destiny, events. Man is by definition the unadjustable being, subduer of earth, and he finds himself at home in the characterization. The ancients who first wrote it down did not get it from surveys and statistics; they looked into their own hearts.

People, especially wives, imagine a wandering husband is temporarily obsessed by other company, but that somewhat misstates the case. Love heightens one's sense of particularity, of being somebody, and one strength of a mistress is her paradoxical gift of restoring native loneliness. For this a man gives up an empire and sails the open sea. To measure him against charts or other men's performance, as if he were in a police lineup or a bug under a microscope, attacks his very nature. For all their rhetoric, the Victorians knew one thing moderns do not: that life is lived by one person at a time, amid particular events, and has genuine importance only where it imparts this distinctiveness to the one who lives it.

How is it that we sell out so cheaply to "science"? There are limits to one's energy, after all. A passion for explanation leaves little to expend on love—and I do not mean only sex. Wives might be amazed to know how much time a mistress spends listening; cooking favorite dishes; selecting a gift or her own clothes to please; developing her knowledge of many things from medieval art to fly-casting; seeking out new places to go; *caring*.

Marriage is unquestionably more convenient than a love affair, and that in itself ought to warn a wise woman against letting it become a mere convenience, like a car pool or membership in a good club. Being a mistress is on the whole rather inconvenient, bad for society, bad for one's creature aspects—children, a home, security, old age—and this inconvenience is part of its attraction. The heritage of two thousand years has inclined us to want more than being effective units of the public weal.

The lonely cry in all of us not to be nothing, to make some sign upon the universe, is not answered by proprieties. Alfred North Whitehead listed adventure as one of five necessities to the truly civilized community, next after truth and beauty, ahead of art and peace. It is a startling idea and he meant it to be so. Men and women are both taught to recognize adventure only as a passing fancy in the growing child, to be put aside with adolescence at the latest. The mature individual settles down; that is to say he does without adventure. Then he should do without beauty, and faith, and laughter, for these too are incidental to "real life", to eating and begetting and keeping out of the rain. This is what life is all about, it is said, and a romance is artificial precisely because it escapes such utilitarian cares. I am not so sure. For one thing, it doesn't escape them; no human situation does. A hermit in a tree house has his daily necessities, and so has a love affair, though they are usually of a different order than in marriage.

And again, what is real life? If man does not live by bread alone, neither does he by a paycheck and enough insurance and coming home on the 5:17 each day. Wives too easily identify husbands and even themselves by their functions, but the mechanics of living are not living. They are like a stage set; if it is effective, the audience applauds when the curtain goes up, and it then recedes into the background as the drama unfolds. By itself the *mise en scène* is no substitute for dialogue and action, in a play or in reality.

Adventure is as needful to the real life of the spirit as food is to the body. The inadvisability of an action will not curtail it if it fills that need. Gambling is more or less bad for society, but people will play the tables so long as hope of sudden wealth connotes hope of change, variety. That is why it appeals broadly to the poor more than the rich: their lives are drearier. Workers go on strike not only for wages and decent hours but out of sheer dramatic hunger. A love affair imparts adventure, not merely because it is unsanctioned and a little risky, but because it proceeds on part-knowledge, like all creative endeavor. A general goes into battle; an artist paints; men climb Everest and fling themselves into the sky; become healers, and judge a crime on part-knowledge. They have to, for that is the condition of living. I do not claim a love affair is nobler or better than marriage; usually it is not. But often an affair is more congenial to human nature. Men must be bold or die inside, and nobody was

27

ever bold without being sometimes wrong. Marriage produces its own downfall when it tries to prevent boldness and sew up the future, and hope, and daring, in a bag.

Men are quite factual when they say a mistress has nothing to do with the way they feel about their wives, and both women do well to understand that. A man may not want his marriage torn up for the same reason that he does not want his job restructured; it upsets the framework within which over the years he has come to operate easily and skillfully. But that doesn't mean he loves his wife at all or his mistress not enough. They are simply not on the same plane. It is possible for them to coincide in one person, the wife; possible but rare because society assumes a mistress is in the wrong and therefore has nothing to say to a woman in the right. But she does.

Being Loved

A successful mistress knows how to be loved; it seldom occurs to a wife that it is necessary to learn. Many people believe that being loved follows inevitably from loving, but that is not so. Few things could be more misleading than the modern precept, solemnly served up with scientific and ecclesiastical cresses, that the way to be loved is—just to love. It looks so appetizing and, like mushrooms, can be deadly. In the first place, it cannot be willed like that; nobody loves merely because it is said to be a good thing to do. In the second place, it promotes self-righteousness, surely the least lovable of characteristics. Third, it smacks of manipulation: Love, and you shall be loved back; it's all a matter of playing the game, nobly of course, but still a *quid pro quo*, which it is exactly love's province not to be. Fourth, it won't work. There is nothing more distressing than being desired by someone one is not attracted to, whether it is a child, a friend, a colleague, or a lover, and the more fervent the suit, the cooler one grows. By what possible logic would it work in reverse? If I were God, I should not answer importunate prayers, precisely because they so sublimely misconceive the situation. A stubborn ardor is plain tyranny, hot to coerce appreciation. It is like the sham generosity of people who say, "I must share this with you"—meaning never a loaf of bread or a hundred dollars but an idea or an emotion, as if one were incapable of one's own. What they really seek is a pleased and astonished audience. Reciprocation is not caused by the intensity of one's own feeling, no matter how pure, but by the willingness and power to receive.

This does not mean the love in one's own heart is worthless, only that it is no guarantee of response, and the giddy notion that it ought to be will spoil and corrupt even its own goodness. If there is a secret to being loved it lies in *not having to have it*. It is this ability a mistress must accommodate or choose some other style of life; while a wife can default it until the day she finds herself living in a hollow tree, and then it is too late. I do not say a

34

mistress always achieves her self-possession lightly or in full confidence; if she does it stridently or in shame, it is artifice. But what is done with a heavy heart, if it is true and good, can also teach and enlighten. Once she assimilates the fact that were the love affair to end, she herself would survive and make a life, although never the same again, she has the ground and power to be loved, almost to command it.

Those are the terms upon which life is given, not alone to mistresses but more immediately discernible in their case. Love is natural to us and quite likely essential, but the hard truth is that no one love is indispensable. We may not like it but it must be faced, else we are children playing house, pretending emotions we have not yet grown into. A recent widower said to me, after thirty-five years of a notable marriage, "I would not have believed it six months ago, but that chapter is finished—and the book goes on."

Human beings meet for a moment in the reaches of time and space, trailing sparks like comet's hair, but we belong to ourselves. We are all required at last to accept full responsibility for our own events and conditions, and only so long as we evade it, crying after some other arrangement, are we fragmented, lost, unquiet, and unloved. The men and women who see this fact without blinking, and set out to master it, are the most attractive people on earth. They will always be loved, whether they will it or not, because they have learned how.

Self-pity is never justified, and a mistress discovers it early because her whole position is somewhat anomalous. She has, as the saying goes, only herself to blame. The edict is just, and society, which decrees it, cannot arbitrarily rescind its other half: the credit is hers as well—and there is always some credit even in wrongfulness so long as it is lived responsibly; that is to say, so long as one lives up to the bargain one has made. The liability clause in the unwritten contract a mistress makes with society contains excellencies which neither society nor the woman may expect.

A wife is apt to feel that imperfections in her marriage are due to catastrophe or some misjudgment or perversity. A mistress accedes to shadows from the start, or must give up the situation altogether, and she finds, to her unfathomable delight, that the dark places do not make love treacherous or false. Rather, the shadows are one phase of a deeply significant cycle that scientists are just beginning to comprehend, a wholeness that pervades all living. A mistress is brought into congruity with this cycle, which is what I meant by feeling linked to all the universe. Those who would know authentic love must yield to all its components; if half-love is enough, it is safe to leave out darkness.

A mistress always knows more than she says to anyone—to other women, to the man in her life, even to herself. A good woman friend is a marvel, and at times it is wisdom to air one's brains; it unheats them. But a woman who habitually complains against a man is quibbling. Either live with him, and hold your tongue, or act, but don't harp, unless you really mean to keep from being loved. High praise is no better taste or any less fatal. Nobody wants his virtues advertised. A liaison has discretion imposed upon it, but a marriage license is not a permit for publicity.

Nor does a mistress attempt to reveal all her mind to the man concerned. I heard a psychiatrist tell a class of medical internes that that impulse to "tell all" was one sure sign of being in love, but he was mistaken. It is a sign of inexperience and uncertainty, a child's effort to catch a sunbeam. I know what the psychiatrist meant: that love is a tenuous line of communication we seek at once to substantiate in words and claims, but words are unruly stuff. They can overwhelm the bond instead of confirming it.

When she is young—in years or in events—a mistress may long like other women to pour out her heart, but circumstances heap against her mental doors like windblown leaves. Her own pride or sense of fitness makes her chary of words like "love" or "always," and the situation does not lend itself to confessions. One goes slowly. There are subtle but precise boundaries at which she must stop if the affair is to go on. She does not ask nosy questions about the man's other life, and if he talks to her of it, she forestalls his saying things he will regret. Happiness built upon malediction is negative and counterfeit, and she knows it. Such restrictions may sound suffocating, but in fact the opposite is true, like the discipline in art that alone releases its force and molds style. Initially, a mistress may inwardly rebel, but one day she surprises herself by preferring the restraint.

I have spent all my professional life dealing in words—not my own; other people's, but still making ideas articulate. It was one of Matthew's special joys. We could talk for hours, and did, but it was talk that went some place, not private chatter. That was the hallmark of its worth, but I did not yet know that, and sometimes I felt I should explode with unsaid thoughts. We would chase one another's minds over a play we had just seen, like dogs romping in the snow; or toss literary allusions back and forth until we ended up laughing and exhausted; or argue politics and talk shop end-lessly—and never say aloud our care for each other. He had a way of pressing one thumb against my cheek, like a potter's imprint... It was almost im-possible sometimes not to speak, but instinct told me to wait; a day would come for words.

And it did: in a chalk-white house in Mexico with a piñon fire and thick Oaxaca rugs on the tiled floor. Two mountain-high weeks away from the world, wrapped by the gentle ferocity of Indians who wished us well, knowing all they needed to of our lives by instinct and swift senses, without lan-guage. I could have said then whatever I wished, but the urgency was removed along with the world that nourished it. It had no more substance there than a dream; I would have been a fool to concoct it for my vanity.

We went back soon enough but the terrible necessity for words did not, for I knew now we were living it into reality, every day. Matthew knew its ranges as well as I, as the Indians had known us both without a tedious telling. I was enchanted and my first impulse was to tell him *that*, but I checked in time and laughed aloud. When he asked me what was funny, I said, "I am. The world. Us," and he was pleased and let it go at that, not disclosing all his thinking, either. When what is said arises from what is lived, words contain more than they say; but when speaking is the substance rather than the vehicle, it soon becomes hollow.

Speech, like fire, is a gift from the gods, and I do not extol dumbness. But total recall is a *clinical* process, and nothing is more chilling to affection. Thoughts and feelings, like other living things, need time and shelter in which to shape themselves. A wife is much mistaken who pries at her husband's mind as if it were an oyster she would eat for dinner, or spreads her own before him in a torrent. A mistress, because she has few stated rights, learns restraint; a wife, having almost too many, is tempted to usurp.

There is another need for reserve, a decent *sotto voce* in talking to oneself. Being loved does not demand mental censorship, but it requires a certain pruning of one's thoughts. An emotional debauch is not greatness of feeling. Second-guessing, agonizing, leaping to unwarranted conclusions are killers of the dream. A mistress who let her mind run riot on such fripperies would be dispossessed next week. She accepts more than she attempts to explain or justify. If the time comes when she can no longer acquiesce, then that is a new situation calling for a new decision, but until then she does not torture the relationship by constant scrutiny. There are a dozen valid reasons why any love affair should not exist, so that reasoning about it, pro or con, is at least contradictory. But all love is a lingua franca not reducible to grammar, married love included.

Explaining love is like explaining poetry. Critics do it all the time, after the poem comes into being, and may do it brilliantly and right. But it never, ever, turns the critic into a poet nor evokes a single new poem from those who know how to make them. Robert Frost said a poem "begins in delight and ends in wisdom." So does love, and not all the theorists with scales and surveys and half-sciences can make it go the other way: begin with wisdom and finish in delight.

Love is not a ready-made value floating in space; it exists in human beings, taken one-to-one. Men and women—or rather a man and a woman—invent love as they go; it cannot be determined by pre-conditions. A woman who argues with herself, "If he loved me, he would spend more time with me," or "buy me presents," or "cater to my needs," is practicing not to be loved. What such polemics mean is that if he had a nicer character, she could love him more, and how dare he be so undeserv-

41

ing? If she has married a rogue, that can be too bad or exciting, but it is no criterion of affection. A scoundrel may know more of actual love than the pinchpenny personality without gumption to fling itself into any venture.

Have a care for the loose talk inside your head. It reflects in a hundred subtle ways: a tone of voice, a glance, a gesture, the things you choose to laugh at, the quickness or slowness of response. All this in turn governs the quality and amount of love you will allow, and thus the kind you get. I do not say a mistress is above these same mistakes, only that she does not keep making them over and over; she doesn't get the chance.

It is critical to understand that intelligence and love do not blockade one another. I have know men and women both married and not, who all their lifetime have borne the grief of not knowing real love, and yet they keep the word abstract. They expect love to be a mystical magical something unrelated to whatever other powers they may have. They never examine their own natures, or what might be demanded of them if love arrived tomorrow. They carry in their heads a line from bad novels: "If you have to think about it, it isn't love." Nonsense. That is like saying if you have to study, it is not talent. There is no point in beseeching heaven for a miracle one would not recognize if one met it at high noon. What is vague and cloudy to the intellect is apt to remain vague and cloudy in experience, even as the eye cannot readily see what the mind does not credit. The eye outside the microscope, for example, rarely sees anything, although it may be wide open and looking.

One excellent way to hamper being loved is the grandiose scheme to love everybody. Taken in its proper sense, this can be a brave goal, but misconstrued it does great damage. I am not here going to argue the proper sense; scholars have been trying to do that for centuries. The difference between the Greek *agape* and *philia*, both translated into English as *love*, is a topic for a Plato to expand upon. But of two points I am sure: love in this context is other than man-woman polarity, although ideally they can mingle. And: nowhere in the Bible is it recommended to love the world *en masse*. Erotic love of everybody is indeed forbidden, as it is in any society. Christ Jesus admonished his followers to love one other, and one's neighbor—in the singular, please note. He made plain that the most unlikely people could qualify as a neighbor under certain circumstances, but that is a far cry from indiscriminate engulfment of the entire human race. He himself was exceedingly selective.

As for being loved by everyone, the very idea is exhausting. A settled good will toward humanity is an adult and great-hearted disposition, but one of love's consummate powers is exclusivity. It provides the human spirit with a place of its own, a locus as necessary as knowledge of its own identity. Diffused affection, loving the whole world, requires much less commitment than loving one man or woman at close range; these are not even emotions of the same order. Love is particularity and a mistress knows it well. A wife forgets it in a welter of children and relatives and the community—all legitimate concerns but secondary and to be kept in their place.

One of this country's legendary tycoons, with three only slightly less dazzling brothers, once told me a factor in their success was the knowledge that their parents loved each other more than they loved the children. They were an impoverished immigrant family and the boys worked hard from the age of seven. They were severely punished in the manner of those days, even whipped on rare occasions. Yet each grew up to command a great enterprise. "People say that loving children enough will stop juvenile crime," the businessman said, "but I don't know what that means. You can love a child out of all balance, and that's going to warp

44

him. We knew that our father came first with our mother, and she with him, and that to a child is strength. It is a little like knowing you are born of royal blood, at once a privilege and a challenge. We were somebody, princelings of a great power, and we knew it and put down roots in it."

If you would be loved, don't help. Too many wives fancy the role of aide to their husband's careers, and are dismayed and stunned when it is not appreciated. Any man worth his salt wants to get there on his own volition. He can hire assistants without incurring emotional obligations. The cliché of the successful man who discards the wife who helped him climb there is both a truism and a rough justice. In a way his leaving her is almost as necessary as his going out from his mother's help at an earlier stage, and a wife who overdoes her assistance may make it as inevitable. Being a power behind the throne is a field where heads roll more frequently than not. It takes more skill than direct ambition for oneself, and skills of a kind that work against love: concealment, politics, knowing too much.

Driving women are found more frequently in the middle to upper echelons of society where there is something to be gained besides money, some reflected prestige, power, attention. This hints the

45

fact that a wife's motives in helping her husband may not be as pure as she likes to think. The wives of truck drivers and electrical repairmen rarely expect to share credit for their husbands' advancement, but they are not immune to the dangers of trying to help. I know intimately of two such marriages that were destroyed in the great depression. In one case the wife went to work, not because she wanted to, but, as she said repeatedly, "to help Joe out." A wife who worked through choice was somehow failing as a woman, but to help one's husband had a lofty sound. The other woman tried to bolster her unemployed husband's spirits, assuring him his work was good and would be marketable again, when he knew she had no basis at all for judging. He needed to hear it from other men who knew his trade, and her saying it out of blind love was only salt in a wound—without its healing properties. Both marriages broke up.

One of the best marriages I have ever witnessed—and it lasted over forty years—was based in part upon the clearheadedness of the husband who, when still a bridegroom, took his wife's hands and said, "My dear, I love you, and I want to have a home and children with you, and a 'meeting of true minds,' but leave-my-work-alone!"

That man was just beginning a brilliant future as a playwright, and his wife had nurtured dreams of opening nights with herself in a mink coat, being coaxed onstage to share a bow. She saw herself bringing coffee and sandwiches on a tray to the study, and instead discovered he worked in a small grubby office that was virtually off-limits. When occasionally she picked him up there, she had to stand while she waited; there were no extra chairs. Once she told him the place was cold, and he yelled, "I like it that way!" When his greatest play was published in book form, he dedicated it, "To my wife because she never interferes."

She laughed and said to me, "I never expected *that* to be my accolade, but I'm proud of it now."

It does not follow that a woman ought to be a hindrance, nor that a deep love does not help a man to his full powers of expression, in his work as elsewhere. But that is by the way; we have got it backward when we insist that love causes personality—in raising children, in marriage, in teaching, in any relationship. Character comes first; without the person there could be no love or exchange of any kind.

The whole idea of help connotes a degree of helplessness, corrosive in its inception. One helps children or the elderly, the sick, the poor, those reeling under the blow of tragedy, but unless such assistance is conscientiously temporary, it makes for a neurotic situation on both sides. A man succeeds in spite of his mistress, and she may even constitute some danger to his aims. Thus he can bring his triumphs to her in full panoply of his own honor, no quarter asked or given.

Two wives who have always irritated me are fictional, but it is the business of drama to show us sudden truth. One is Candida in Bernard Shaw's play of the same name; the other is James Barrie's Maggie in *What Every Woman Knows*. I have seen only one production of the latter; that was quite enough of Maggie for me, a gray mouse no one suspected of being the brains of her brilliant husband. *Candida* is much the better work, and Shaw was such a rascally knave, I've never been certain whether he meant his heroine to appear marvelous or baneful. I suspect he wanted audiences to betray themselves by their choice, and I freely admit to detesting the woman. Beautiful, charming, intelligent, she regards all males with what Shaw calls "an amused maternal indulgence," reducing her husband to an eldest child and wrecking his manhood. He is a clergyman, and the couple have befriended a shy and poetic erstwhile student about half Candida's age, who falls wildly in love with her. Like a knight of old, he keeps his distance, only plying her with poetry and art, but he stings the pedantic husband into an argument that exposes his cardboard assumptions.

Candida intervenes, naturally, and defends her ineffectual mate, saying, "Look at this other boy here—my boy—spoiled from his cradle. We go once a fortnight to see his parents... You know how strong he is—how clever he is—how happy. Ask James's mother and his three sisters what it cost to save James the trouble of doing anything but be strong and clever and happy. Ask me what it costs to be James's mother and three sisters and wife and mother to his children all in one... Ask the tradesmen who want to worry James and spoil his beautiful sermons who it is that puts them off. When there is money to give, he gives it: when there is money to refuse, I refuse it. I build a castle of comfort and indulgence and love for him, and stand sentinel always to keep little vulgar cares out. I make him master here, though he does not know it, and could not tell you a moment ago how it came to be so. And when he thought I might go away with you...he offered me his strength for my defense, his industry for my livelihood, his position for my dignity—ah, I am mixing up your beautiful sentences and spoiling them, am I not, darling?"

To this her husband, as spineless as spaghetti, kneels and replies, "It's all true, every word. What I am you have made me with the labor of your hands and the love of your heart. You are my wife, my mother, my sisters: you are the sum of all loving care to me."

Candida, satisfied, purrs at the horrified poet, whose heart and idol are equally shattered, "Am I your mother and sisters to you, Eugene?"

"Ah, never!" he cries in disgust.

Here I always want to break out flags and blow trumpets. I share the young man's disgust. Candida offers him a parting homily, helper to the last, with which to comfort himself that it would never have worked: she is after all fifteen years older. To that he retorts, "In a hundred years, we shall be the same age." He leaves, and the curtain falls as the married couple embrace. In today's crisp lingo, they deserve each other. Candida could never have been a mistress; she had neither the imagination nor the courage. She did not love a man, she wouldn't have known what to do with one; she loved herself and her position as prime mover. Certainly she had no idea how to *be* loved. The crudest injury inflicted on love is administration.

Wives and mistresses have different clocks. A wife can become so engrossed with the future that she almost ceases to live today. Everything is for tomorrow: the children's education, the bigger house, next year's promotion, retirement, the long focus upon some event not yet arrived. A mistress lives perhaps too much in the present, but this very immediacy, physical and spiritual, is a lodestar. More than one man has said, or thought, that with his mistress he at least knows himself alive. The present is all that really can be known, and though it is perceived in blocks of time, not moments, dragging around the future wears upon it as much as dragging around the past. Anybody with common sense looks a little to where he is going, but not so much as to mortgage the present to a dubious some day. Spontaneity coexists with a love affair, but marriage does not have to be a rigidly planned economy. A young widow struggling to make ends meet said to me, "I'm glad every day for all the reckless things we did. If we had waited till we could afford them, now it would be too late."

A mistress perceives that love is not calibrated in length of days but in height and depth. A love affair is constantly subject to two threats: a foreseeable end and a fragmentary present, which ought to destroy it but they don't. On the contrary, they intensify the mood, not factitiously but in recognition of humanity's covenant with time. Marriage cannot extort foreverness from the everywhere present law that "all things are fleeting, nothing is our own." A love affair does not ask security against the world's fate; it shares that fate and knows it only too poignantly, which gives it great vitality for its season.

Love cannot undo the laws by which all things live, and a whimpering insistence that it do so is infantile babbling. Love endures not in a perpetual day, but in the reality of having seen and touched and known, an alchemy that changes forever one's relationship to time. Love will never hold back the dark, but it is so blazing a truth that it compensates for transience. Married lovers would do well to remember that; the unmarried have no choice.

Part of falling in love is the heady blend of familiarity and strangeness. Here is someone at once so like you that you have come home, and yet so different he opens a thousand windows on the universe. Love needs both aspects to endure.

A man I know returned from war duty on unexpected leave to find his wife of nine years living with another man. Stunned and furious, he threw the man out, bodily, and then walked away himself without looking back. Months passed while he delayed action on the pending divorce, and when I asked him why (he is young enough to be my son), he said, "I know it doesn't make sense. I'm through—there's no doubt in my mind about that. Only I would have sworn I knew that woman down to her fingertips, and the fact that I obviously didn't makes me—well, half-attracted again. She's like a stranger."

If you would stay loved, stay strange a little. Maintain a reserve of mind and heart, not a sly withholding but the privacy of personality. That is neither self-indulgence nor a conjuror's trick; it is a clause in one's moral contract with existence. There is no valid excuse to resign from living, or to get one's perceptions secondhand, or to shirk the hard job of finding out who one is or may become. Marriage inevitably contracts one's horizons in some measure. One is no longer looking, for example, for a mate—all the more cause to look in other directions, up and over and around. The future is less questionable—very well, go question art, or history, or whatever else captivates your spirit. That is what a spirit is for, and it is now free to search in other realms. A major reason for ordering life is to liberate one's energies for their real work. Marriage is one kind of ordering, and that by no means belittles marriage but esteems it, as the Japanese flower arranger treats the string and paper that enwrap his flowers with the same meticulous care he gives the blossoms. But a wife who falls in love with the ordering process, as if that in itself filled up life's purposes, smothers her marriage in logistics.

Matthew once said to me, in a fit I suppose of home-grown annoyance, though I did not ask, "If you ever want me to leave you, do housework." He did not mean it didn't have to be done; he meant not to make it the focus of our lives. Nor did he mean housework alone; he meant triviality of any kind. A wise wife cultivates at least one field to her liking and sows new seed in it continually. If children and household suffer somewhat from it, that cannot be avoided. Both will suffer far more if the marriage bogs down in monotony and indifference. I am not saying a man wanders after another woman for her good mind, and yet in an important sense he does—unless he is a Don Juan or some other kind of adolescent, and that is a different matter.

A mind arched against its own segment of sky is as lovely as a body doing so. It would never occur to a mistress that keeping her mind clothed and working was dangerous to her romance; quite the opposite is true. A mind that has achieved some craftsmanship is self- contained, not greedy; it has learned the value of waiting and knows when not to wait; it has attained the grace of the easy gesture, and a blend of pride and peace. This achievement doesn't have to be of genius caliber. I have seen it in women making bread, weaving, gathering grapes, binding books, packing parachutes—crooning to them as they might have sung lullabies to infant sons. Some intellectual mastery is fundamental to lasting love because it is fundamental to personality, and it is at least difficult to love a non-person.

Mistresses are not glamorous creatures who never have to sweep a floor or mend; they are surprisingly domestic. I have never known one who was not a superb cook, or did not have a good deal of house pride and take pleasure in entertaining well. Yet all such daily ministry is muted, not merely in deference to others but in justice to herself. It is not only that a man does not like housework going on under his feet; *she* does not think it is the biggest thing in life. Life comes as daily usage even to heads of state and great artists; they too must have clean socks and a cup of coffee, and sometimes must provide it for themselves. But menial necessities are not a reason to be living, and energies tied down to such service are blinded from perceiving even that they are tied.

There is no need to make heavy weather of keeping house, or even of raising children, and only a mind otherwise unengaged would whip up a storm around it. A wife does not have to be a career woman, but she does need to be a woman, whole person with brain and hands. One is born female, but being a woman is a personal accomplishment.

My grandmother was half-Spanish and lived on a ranch the size of a county. She could deliver a baby and halter-break a colt, and play a guitar, and dance at the governor's ball in an embroidered white silk gown. When her oldest friend died, my grandmother was eighty-seven. At the church she walked alone and silent down the aisle and laid a wild iris in the coffin to say good-by, stirring four hundred people to tears. A reporter wrote of her, and her dead friend, "These were the great women of the West. They don't make them like that any more."

I suppose he was right, but what a waste and what a pity. There is a world out there as much as ever, a portion of which each man and woman is born to inherit. To turn away from it is to deny some part of one's own personality. A hundred years ago it was the mistress who imagined the world well lost for love, and this insularity in the long run undermined the illicit affair. Today it is more often the wife who renounces everything for home and family, and fails to see that it is not giving so much as giving up. It may indeed be more worthy to give than to receive, but who can give with empty hands? We all start from the same basis of nakedness and ignorance, and must increase by receiving whatever we have the capacity to receive from the torrential universe. Take what is given, respect it, exult in it, multiply it: that is a law as an old man, for then and only then shall you have anything worth giving back. Study something, learn something, risk more than you think you can, care something, become something—if in truth you wish to be loved.

Who Are You?

Who Are You?

*W*hen I used to exclaim, as, infrequently, I could not help doing. "You make me very happy!" Matthew did not often let me get away with it. He would reply quietly, "You make yourself happy. I am simply part of it." That half pleased me with its scent of wisdom, for stirring my mind awake was characteristic of his impact; and half alarmed me with its hint—as I felt, so foolishly are we taught—that our love was illusionary. Another time he said, "Don't lay such a burden on me, unless you want to kill this lovely thing. If you were on a desert island, you'd find reasons for happiness because it is your nature. I don't mean you are incapable of sorrow, but you are not a morose personality, don't you see?"

I was beginning to. Without telling me like a giddy sophomore to define my terms, he was Socratic in his approach to life.

At last he rebuked me kindly. "Say that you are happy—that pleases me; but not that I make you so. Your happiness is not mine to give or withhold and I decline to have it. That would falsify all our dealings."

I knew truth when I saw it, as most minds do, and I never again told him he made me happy. That may sound literal-minded and paltry, but the reverse I think is the case. Carelessness in perceiving what one means leads to carelessness in the meaning. I could easily have fallen into the premise that it was Matthew's business to make me happy. His business was to be himself, whole person, with or without me, as it was mine to accomplish my being. Only out of this is anything like love possible.

I have come to believe that love is not so much an event as a disposition, not something forthcoming from others but within one's own power to pour out. We deserve the kind and amount of love we get, not in any moralistic sense but by the quality of our being. The only people worth loving are those who are determined to find life good whether you love them or not. The bubble belief that dumping one's happiness on another enhances affection is merely shirking. Emerson said God offers to every mind the option between truth and repose, but not both. The same choice has to be made between love and laziness.

In the nature of things, we meet and marry long before we are full-scale identities, but that is no excuse for staying incomplete. We love most those who make us fulfill whatever greatness lies in us, not those who induce us to resign it. Remember how it was at first, how you went around pouring out; and refill your reservoir from the same springs as before you met, for that is what brought love to your door.

Marriage is often an attempt to bring life as nearly to a standstill as possible, guaranteeing what no one can: to go on feeling a certain way. Swearing to love forever is like promising to feel perpetually any other emotion, fear or sorrow, admiration or joy. Some thinkers argue that this inability is the cause and reason for marriage existing at all, a decent provision for stability after love has fled. Perhaps; but it seems to me a dreary and doubtful prospect, diminishing love to a kind of bank holiday. What one can swear is to go on being worth loving, a vow that is more flexible, more attainable, and more true.

A working love affair has its humdrum stretches and sieges of anger, as does marriage, but on each side of an affair there is some place one can go, geographically and emotionally. This allows strength and grace to both partners; there is not the frightful attrition of one personality upon another. If, after a serious break, a man and his mistress find each other again, it is not reconciliation but a new encounter upon a different plateau. In this respect, it is akin to an intense friendship between two men who, in occasionally battling each other, go on separate journeys and return with more of themselves accomplished.

At one time Matthew and I were at odds for several months, never quite parting but with the spangled air sullied and sere. We both grieved, and I flung at myself all the reproaches one soaks up willy-nilly in a Grundyian world, seeking the entropy of stock judgments. If you had been married, my silly heart began—but my mind balked. It would have happened anyway, and quite probably sooner. What petty grievance was this to snatch away my good sense and happiness? What we had, we had; it was not less for being mortal like all earthly things. I would do it over again without a second's hesitation. Seeing that, I walked a green earth again, and that same day Matthew called to ask if I were free for dinner. We went to a small French restaurant run by a family, and with the first glass of wine, he looked straight at me and said, "A good year to us."

Until that moment I had forgotten it was a private anniversary, nor known on his part or my own whether there would be others. We smiled, dividing a thought.

If love is a creative stuff, it is for that very reason not a continuous state, any more than genius works at gale force every hour. All creative energy has winters and summers, planting and harvest with time between for growth. Love wears a thousand masks, in the literal configuration of *persona*, a sounding through, in no way false but able to change form like any god. "At times," Martin Buber said, "it is like a light breath, at times like a wrestling bout." Buber knew that love is a coming and going, not an unremitting present. He used the word "meeting" to identify true encounter, and the word connotes motion, advancing and receding. One reclaims oneself again and again, and turns and meets the other again, for both are wonderful and both necessary.

If marriage is to be saved from its dead seas, a way shall have to found for wives to have money of their own—legitimately, that is to say as a result of production. Only slaves and very young children are without a source of income. We pour billions of dollars into destitute countries, knowing that prolonged poverty grinds the spirit to dust, but an American wife can whistle. She may spend the lion's share of the nation's wealth, but she does it on sufferance, which varies widely from one husband to the next, and even if it did not, it would still be sufferance.

Without money clearly her own, a wife is not free to act, and moral freedom is nothing else. There is no quicker death to one's feeling of being somebody than impotence to make some portion of one's dreams come true. Where there is no power to act, all equality and education are emptiness. Today a wife can live, approved and encouraged by society, consuming goods and services without having to produce very much in return—a fair description of neurosis. Oh yes, she may be called upon for minimal duties, but these are largely physical, requiring her bodily presence in bed, at parties, or when the children get home from school, and they are negative in that they respond strictly to demand. If no one is there to dinner, she need not prepare it. In a curious inversion, it is she who is bought and paid for; a mistress has more dignity and fairer fortune.

The day of the kept woman is gone forever. A mistress as a rule has to earn her living, and she would not have it any other way. It gives her the self-possession and stature of independent survival, which is a plain goal of life and, in adults, a powerful attraction: dependency, no matter how construed, is simply not grown up. More, it removes from her any slightest taint of having to intrigue for profit, which is ruinous to love. It is shocking how many wives regard gerrymandering as a basic domestic skill, though who can say what one would stoop to if one had no income? I always had, even when I was married, so the position is difficult for me to imagine. I do not say a woman's money makes finance irrelevant. Money enters into every human association from schoolboys buying pastries on their way home to foreign ministers at a conference; it is moonraking to pretend otherwise. But I do say a sharp imbalance of money hinders free relationship, forcing it to make do on what the poorer partner can afford, else turning that one into a sycophant.

Ovid pointed out that Eros was a naked cherub without pockets in his skin to stuff with gain. It is more than just pleasant to buy a man a gift with money that did not, one way or another, come from his own hand. It corresponds to a polarity between

the sexes reaching beyond legal or social "equality," a creative tension where each is whole, yet
each is more because of the other. I should not
dream of marrying without some clear provision
for my own money. There are a dozen workable
ways; all it takes is a little ingenuity and total con-
viction.

If a man has wealth or property when he mar-
ries, he can settle a suitable sum on his wife which
should then become wholly hers. A famous rich
man once gave his new wife a million dollars and
said sternly, "Now that is your capital, you manage
it. Don't come to me about it, don't tell me what
you do with it." Having earned his fantastic wealth
himself, he knew that money is not only freedom, it
is a demand for judgment and control from the one
who holds it, in short for attaining a fuller stature.
Most couples don't operate at such dizzy heights,
but one satisfactory thing about money is that its
principles are the same, whether the amount is five
hundred dollars or five hundred million.

A wife may be given an allowance, however
modest, for which she is accountable to no one.
This is not a handout; it is fully earned. The usual
arrangement is for the wife to work, even if only a
part-time, and to utilize the income commensurate
with the household, the husband's salary, and so

on. One wife I know tutors students, banking executives, and oil company employees in Spanish without leaving her house, and has made from three to seven thousand dollars every year of her married life. She has used part of it for travel, alone or with a woman friend, and when her children were small, to pay a full-time housekeeper while she was away.

A very young couple of my acquaintance had no capital and the wife did not work, but she knew quite a lot about buying and selling land. Her husband, who had a job, agreed to co-sign a note at the bank as his contribution to her acquiring some money. She used the loan to turn over a property on which she made a good profit. After that she signed her own notes. The methods are many, and the benefits make it worthwhile to find or invent one that fits. A mistress is endowed with these benefits from the beginning. Rich or poor, she is not beholden, and what this does to her relationship has often caused me to wonder if equality with women is not a natural hunger in men. There seems to me to be an instinctive rightness in it quite apart from democratic convention and fair play.

In addition to money, the important factor here is people. The necessities of earning a living bring a mistress a variety of associates, personal and professional, while a wife, especially in the suburbs, confines herself to other wives, like a musician who can play but one piece of music. She has acquaintance among tradespeople, teachers, and a raft of neighborhood children who gratify her by not being her own offspring, but this not *knowing*. What I am talking about is a measure of experience, knowing, in a small way but truly, how it feels to be black or white, a crippled child or an isolatedly brilliant one, a Jew, a poet, an Indian, an alcoholic, a business executive, a college student, a cop, a duchess, a trucker, a baseball player—or a hundred thousand other kinds of people. A willingness to know, even when it hurts; caring; knowing as against tolerating.

It is entirely incidental that color and excitement rub off on one from such knowing, though they do. What is far more central is the habit it ingrains of seeing into and out from a different window, another set of eyes and ears; of actually participating for a moment—it is always only that—in another life. That is what love is, or I am wholly ignorant of it.

From my earliest childhood I was taught a modest knowledge of things Chinese, and have always had some affinity for the culture—the food, the poetry, the philosophy, the language—though I

70

am far from being a scholar. One day during the Second World War, I was lunching in San Francisco's Chinatown with Matthew, who held the naval rank of lieutenant commander, desk-and-plane-bound though he was, pleased to be in uniform. It was one of those cobalt blue days in early summer, and as we emerged into Sacramento Street we met a lieutenant general of the Chinese Army, accompanied by another man in civilian dress. The general was easily six feet tall, very thin, and wore his kepi and red collar flashes as though he were born to them, but I did not think he was. There was too much suffering in his face. Matthew saluted instantly and the general returned it with military punctilio underlaid with humanity: a certain acknowledgment as men. Then he looked me full in the face, and with a courtesy four thousand years in the making, bowed, scarcely breaking his stride. It drew from me an echoing gravity, and I too bowed in an oriental fashion that would have been pure fake in any other context; it astonished me that I knew how to do it. It was like encountering Rembrandt or Shakespeare in the flesh—no, not that, for I knew a little of those men's minds; this Chinese was wholly strange, and for an instant wholly seen. I saw what he was seeing, including the woman passing on the street who would in another second become again myself.

Here was meeting, in Buber's special application. For a split second we met across impossible barriers, and recognized and honored—and loved—one another, and let it go; and the mark it made will remain so long as either of us lives. Matthew and I walked on in silence, for he knew and respected what had occurred, and, like me, he was glad to have been there. There is no greed nor vanity in these things, just a pure satisfaction in their existence. When at last we spoke, it was of something in a shop window.

If she is very foolish, a mistress may complain or pry or weep, but one thing she does not blunder into is competition with the man in her life. Or other men, for that matter. Quite simply, she does not need it; she is too much her own woman. Whatever community status she may have does not stem from her connection with him. It comes from her own work, or from her beauty, her brilliance as a hostess, her hospital service, so that any applause she merits is never at his expense. Nor does the barometer of his fortunes cause her own to rise or fall. Her heart may be disturbed but not her position, for it is either unknown or unacknowledged. This, if the community only knew it, confers upon her a peculiar release from constraint. A mistress, more than other women, can keep her love-life and her self-life distinct, and she thinks of them, as men generally do, as simply aspects of her full identity. What is more, she comprehends completely that a man feels the same way. She may be jealous of his wife, but rarely of his work or achievements. She knows out of her own experience that they do not conflict with her for his mind or heart, and very likely she would not give two pins for a man without dedication to his field. It works both ways: the fully realized personality is what attracts and for mature people, nothing less is desirable.

A mistress discovers in a few weeks' time that love has to hold its own with the rest of the world, and if it cannot, it is a mist and she had better find it out. No woman who is a woman wants a man preoccupied with herself. A mind cannot work utterly alone, not even the monk's, the artist's, the thinker's, much less the lover's; it is a chain reactor and requires the bombardment of other minds. The healthy organism seeks the experiences it needs in order to grow; only those that refuse the seeking turn sour.

That is why a dutiful arrangement for a wife to have Wednesday afternoons off will not do it. Casual shopping or lunch in town with a friend or a visit to the local macaroni factory are busy-work. The "outside interests" endorsed by marriage counselors and psychiatrists are strictly that: outside, peripheral, bootless, and women are not so dumb that they do know the difference. What the mind cries out for is serious work that alone furnishes the risk, the reward, the new experience that a living spirit must have or perish. Pursued for their own sake, these qualities are debased into dilettantism.

A mistress knows this without struggling for it, not because she is natively wiser than a wife but because her circumstances teach her. If she forgets, she is apt to be rather rudely reminded. She is thrown upon her own resources and must frequently entertain herself, and this gives her time to read and think and follow her own pursuits. She soon not only welcomes this but defends it with all the fierceness of the *self*-preserving instinct. The overwhelming blessing of love is not another person but oneself, a sudden seeing, a coming into one's own fullness and capacity. Even what we see in the other is somehow a portion of ourselves. We fall in love, I sometimes think, with the kinds of men we would be if we were men. They are our other, unexpressed self, the man-side of us, as we are their woman-side, their tenderness and sensitivity. This accounts for the completeness one feels in love. Let it be as "other" as it will.

A young wife, when she finds herself in some disagreement or argument with her husband's view, is apt to feel frightened and disloyal. She feels driven to deny and muffle her own opinion, which is harmful for eventually it will burst out some other way. Obviously, there has to be some strong affinity of natures between people who love, but this is not measured in bulk. Two cannot be one, and western marriage would be enriched by abandoning such a false ideal. Without difference, without some spatial distance of spirit, no relationship is possible, no give and take. This is so true and natural that when no "other" is present, we create it by talking to ourselves. Almost all thinking is dialogue, interior conversation. That is why possessiveness and the attempt to extract total concurrence from another stifles loves: it goes against the grain, striking at the difference, the otherness that makes love possible.

Attraction can flare up in almost any situation, but love cannot long endure where there are no selves, no terminals between which the spark can alternate. Anode and cathode, yang and yin, riposte, counterpoint, tension: it is just that simple. "I will demand of thee, and answer thou me." The first two times this challenge was flung down, it was God who said it to Job. The third time, Job turned himself and said it to the Lord. From that point, he was released from his miserable trap. One fancies that God smiled.

Sex

I mislike to write of sex. It makes me uneasy. Oh, I know one is supposed to be able to treat it like any other subject, but the fact remains that it is not any other subject. It is itself, explosive, variant, provocative, and very close to the bone. As, to my mind, it should be. Sex has suffered from exposition, not because those who would study it are malicious, but because to make explicit what is by nature implicit is dangerous and misleading. Like the atom, the moment one observes it closely, it shifts, so that the thing one conscientiously examines is not what actually is. As scientists have learned even in their exacting procedures, the observer is not a cool and remote machine; whether one likes it or not, one's own senses are engaged and what one sees is conditioned by the relationship of those particular senses to the facts being

81

studied. The only way to become entirely impersonal is to be dead, and one then makes a poor observer.

The understanding of sex, like any other comprehension, comes from a series of mental leaps that can never be induced by batteries of facts. One cannot cross-examine Eros; he at once turns into his brother quicksilver and runs out between one's fingers. The Zen Buddhists say if one would find one's hands and feet by inquiring of the neighbors, the issue is already lost. And yet—who can write of love and treat sex as supplemental, or ignore it altogether? Sex is and is not love, somewhat as money is and is not wealth. So then, with a thousand wishes to be somewhere else, I venture upon thin ice. Do not take anything I say into yourself unless it fits some hollow or mold you have scooped out by your own temperament. Help me thus far to be faithful to myself, to you, to our mercurial subject.

It used to be that unmarried women were sheltered by their married sisters from the realities of physical love, both its details and its implications. Now the positions are somewhat reversed. Wives are the naïve, almost the ignorant, ones. It is frequently their experience that is narrower without their recognizing it. They take a smattering of

Freudian psychology as warranty for sex as a fixed fact instead of a continuing relationship, evolving, changing, becoming. They suppose if they bother to think about it, that sex at forty is the same thing it is at twenty, and that is idiotic. What Freud expounded, alas, was not so much sexuality as immaturity. Where there is a failure to achieve adulthood, it will be evidenced in all aspects of life, sex included. But it does not follow that immature sex is any more natural or authentic than immature language or eating habits. Because one can read it does not make one knowledgeable about great literature.

Thirty years ago, a woman I knew primarily in the office asked me to dine with her. Then in her mid-thirties, she was at least ten years younger than I, and not married. Since high school she had been the sole support of her mother, who now had died. What she wanted of me was an opinion about having an affair that held no promise of marriage.

"I know it's childish to *ask*," she said, making a face, "but you see, that's part of my difficulty. So many of my emotions are childish. I've never given them anything to grow on. Everything else aside, I am not sure innocence becomes me at this age, any more than bows in my hair or bobby socks would."

I was enchanted. "My dear, if you can say that, you don't need me to advise you. It's head and shoulders above the sexual intelligence of most of the married women I know. I can only say I should trust instincts like that, if I were you."

Some weeks later I returned from lunch to find a single pale pink camellia on my desk and a card with the two words "Thank you." I saw her in and out of the office after that, but the subject was never mentioned again. It was a matter of simple manners on both our parts. To speak without embarrassment when there is occasion is to be free of outmoded taboos, but gratuitous babbling is not only bad taste, it's hokum. If one has to describe the event aloud to be sure it was wonderful, it probably was not. It is wicked not to tell people there is such a thing as sexual etiquette.

Young girls sometimes talk to me about sex, and when I ask, as I am apt to do if I know their families, "Have you talked about this with your mother?" they are quite shocked. "I couldn't possibly," they say. "Mother's a darling and she taught me the fundamentals, but she doesn't know anything about *life*. How could she? She married Daddy right out of college and she's never looked at another man."

I could have been their grandmother, and such folly in the midst of frankness staggers me. I can only conclude that we knew far more about these matters than today's over-informed and under-discerning generations. They discredit their own senses unless they can be stamped with the approval of some authority. What they seek is neither sex nor love but reassurance. We had much less data and far deeper awareness of our own emotions, even our bodies. One had the prime material within one's reach; who wanted it secondhand? Like Christopher Morley's salty heroine *Kitty Foyle*, at fourteen one's own interior was busy communicating messages. As Kitty said, "It's sweet, the not knowing. No one can tell you till you're ready to be told, and there's damn few who will ever tell you anyhow the silly little things we need... What's the first thing people do when they love each other? They begin to make up a language of their own that doesn't mean anything to anyone else... As soon as you begin to fret and worry about meanings, you've lost that something in you that makes it possible to know them." There is more good sense and true information in that than many textbooks.

In my girlhood nice women were not supposed to enjoy sex, but that was only the official position. What they were supposed to do and what they did were quite different. Mother to daughter, it was handed down to know better. My mother, who would be more than a hundred were she alive today, taught me without fuss a saying that was already old when her mother taught her in the 1880s: "You never really know anything about a man until you have eaten at his table and slept in his bed." My people were circumspect as only the staunch middle class can be, but it never entered their heads that that was too blunt for young female ears.

More, I am certain that the official position was undermined from husband to wife. Even as a quite young child, I occasionally intercepted a look between my father and mother that was unmistakable. I could not have translated it into events, but it was perfectly plain to me that here was a secret man-woman magic that would one day be mine. My mother would not have dreamed of detailing the sex act to us, not for our modesty or hers, but for my father's; by her code, one simply did not do that to a man. But neither did she gloss over its factual existence, its practicalities, power, and loveliness. She taught us that it was woman's prerogative to maintain a certain sexual excitement. She never said that in words—they would have choked her— but it was done by intimation and example.

Once when my middle sister was about fifteen and home from school with a bad cold, my mother caught her pottering about the kitchen in a tired old bathrobe. When she chided Irene with looking like an ill-tied sack of potatoes, my sister protested, "But, Mama, I don't feel good."

"And no wonder," my mother said mildly. "The way you look is enough to turn anyone's stomach, including your husband's if one should be foolish enough to marry you. Come with me, child." She took Irene upstairs and brushed her hair, tying it back with a pink ribbon. Then she wiped her face with lotion-soaked cotton and touched the dry lips with colorless pomade—anything more would of course have been unthinkable. The offending garment was bundled up to be used as rags, and Irene was draped in a second-best robe of Mother's, of quilted silk. She tapped the girl's nose with a forefinger and said, "Now look at yourself."

Irene regarded her image in Mother's long glass and turned around with a radiant face. "Mama, you're right! I feel much better!" My mother gave her a smile and said nothing more. She did not need to. I, at eleven, witnessed all this with considerable awe, feeling admitted to mysteries, and learning that particular one the same time my sister did.

I am opposed to sex education as such. It so fatuously confuses vocabulary with vocation. We are not minds or bodies or sex urges or case histories any more than we are mechanisms for breathing or digesting: we are persons. What sex desperately needs is not education but imagination. By all means let us have the biological facts, but not as if they were the whole truth, and not, in heaven's name, in classrooms and groups. Must it be pointed out that sex is intensely individual? Sex education inevitably becomes sex theory, how one "should" feel, react, think, care. One's own sexuality is representative of the condition in others, and in that sense it is universal, but one experiences oneself, not a theory, no matter how wisely stated. A knowledge of averages and generalities creates an anxiety to prove oneself on the correct side. Nothing could be more puritanical and proscriptive. No wonder modern marriage is afflicted with inward weeping.

If even legal and sanctioned sex was once officially considered a shameful secret, now it is secrecy itself that has become the shame. A decent reticence is suspect; it sins against the public visibility that is mistaken for freedom. Privacy is also antagonistic to the welfare state. How can a nation legislate the greatest good for the greatest number if happiness insists upon remaining private and particular? We have not yet slid over the brink politically, but there is a sociological and psychological totalitarianism that subverts marriage and sex with statistics and compatibility prediction scales. Yet the spirit dies hard, thank goodness, and a love affair is one thing people are still somewhat commended for keeping to themselves, not out of respect for either love or taste but because society does not want its boat rocked. I sometimes think only lovers are free to love; husbands and wives are compressed into roles to be played but not truly lived.

In a controlled and increasingly homogenized social order, sexual expression is narrowed down to one channel, the erotic, so overloading it that it is becoming a burnt out case. The sensual texture of life used to be fulfilled on many levels; sailing, weaving, fire-making, woodworking, cooking; the feel of tools; the handling and gentling of animals; travel that was not trajectory in an air-conditioned capsule; reading; real talk. Now life is so largely a spectator sport that the senses are starved, and it is still true that the devil finds work for idle hands. That is to say, unused energies explode where they can. For many, sex and crime are the only avenues to uniqueness and participation. This accounts in part for the unmotivated crime; as the nihilists knew, destructiveness is a form of initiative when other forms are lacking. One hears it said in defense of the criminal, "At least he acted." And it accounts in part for the exploitation of sex in films, novels, advertising, homosexuality, the faddist use of drugs, too-early marriage, and casual loveless affairs.

When my young friends discuss sex, they speak of it as "being close" to someone, or "having something of my own," or "making me feel special." This betrays an alarming spiritual and sensual void. It is an attempt to extract from sex the sense of unity and continuity that can only be poured into it. Taken in the abstract, sex is in no way glorious. Children, upon first hearing of it, spontaneously regard it as either squalid or absurd, and they are right. It acquires its character from us. Eroticism in or out of marriage cannot endow life with meaning, and sex retains its richness just so long as we bring meaning to it.

It is fraud to infer that sexual understanding comes with the gross facts. The truths of sex are discovered in its subtleties. The most telling erotic scene I have ever witnessed was in a British espionage drama on public television. The man concerned was cooking himself a humble meal throughout; the woman was perched on a kitchen chair in coat and hat, having just arrived. There was no lurid grappling, no bared flesh; it was all done verbally, and even that was below the surface of their actual words. Two strong personalities were at a breaking point in their mutual but unspoken desire, held in check by awareness of powerful circumstances, loyalty to sworn service, the likely risk to other lives if they yielded, personal complications. The outcome walked on a razor's edge, and the viewer ached not for the characters but with them. One's own molecules were in such disarray that when the woman said softly, brokenly—the only outward acknowledgement of what they had been discussing—"I would stay, if I could," and departed, you almost shouted in relief. One more second and you felt the television set would have exploded. That kind of sensual and spiritual faceting alone gives sex its radiance.

When it is new to us, sex provides not only sensations but a hint of wondrous realms beyond sensation, as does any other fresh intelligence. But like other newborn creations—an idea, a baby, a talent, a purpose—it requires to be developed. Sexual poise is not expertise, which is only a kind of proficiency in mechanics, and may remain quite ignorant. Sensation and experience are not identical, and the muddled effort to make them interchangeable is one of the saddest of modern confusions. Feelings always accompany experience but they do not constitute it. That is why any attempt to regain experience merely by repeating the sensation is doomed to failure and bitterness. In the sphere of sex, this results in the empty chase after gratification, else apathetic compliance with incidental physicality, both of which are immoral because they isolate and insult the body. Sexuality today is lonely.

I do not claim being a mistress is the morally superior position; I am trying to show why and how a wife may make a mistress inevitable. Mere legality is cheap. Perfunctory sex is about as immoral as one can get. If I were teaching the young, I should teach them that. Indifference to sex except in its occasional enactment is degrading. The British theoretical physicist Lancelot Whyte has said that sex dissociated from the rest of life is actually anti-organic, anti-human, blunting aesthetic values and destroying its own professed goal: sexual harmony.

A tumult on stage is not dramatic action. More likely it is a cover-up for its absence. In drama, action is development of character or forward movement of the plot. Although action in this stage sense is not always divorced from physical motion, actors can be sitting quite still yet project a regular dynamo of dramatic action. So, too, meticulous adherence to the rules is not necessarily morality, though neither is a sharp infraction, of course. Morality begins in rules and goes on to self-responsibility. It is a gradual integration of myriad forces: desire, self-esteem, loyalty, courage, fitness, awareness, and much else. Morality is for adults; children need rules because they could not possibly cope with the complexities of moral decisions. What the adult learns is that each moral choice is unique and cannot be made alone on the basis of past choices. Life will ultimately make hay of any prefabricated system of thought, and the adult who clings to it anyhow avoids both the rough work of thinking and his own maturity.

Not long ago a sixteen-year-old girl asked me, in tears, if there were two moral codes; one for adults and one for young people. I told her yes, more or less, that one has to earn the right to immorality.

She had just found out her adored father had had a mistress for ten years. "Are you saying that it's perfectly all right for Daddy to do what he did?" she asked.

"I'm saying it may be," I replied. "I don't know him or the circumstances. I'm asking you not to judge him by your standards, which can be both right for you and obsolete for him."

"But I loved him so much. I—I believed in him."

"Yes, but the time has come for you to love your father on a more adult level," I said. "Morality isn't just not doing something, you know. Would you love him more if he were afraid, or lied to you about it?"

She looked at me. "No."

"Let me ask you something else. Why did you come to me? There must be other women you know much better."

"Yes, but you—I have heard you know about these things."

"That didn't disgrace me in your eyes?"

"Oh, no," she cried. "I thought you were the only one who could understand."

"Well, then," I said, "if experience can give me some measure of wisdom, could it not do the same for others? For your father, for example?"

After a moment, she smiled a little. "It's hard work, growing up."

All that glitters is not sex. It can be ego, loneliness, tyranny; and it can be sheer joy or sexual friendship, which is not love but has its own kind of validity. Indeed a woman is fortunate who has had a man treat her as a sexual friend, for it teaches her to know the difference, to realize that sex is not all one tone. I have heard wives say proudly that they do not use sex as a weapon: "I have never closed my door to my husband." And I have wondered in my heart, Why not? Do they not know that monotony is a weapon too? Are they merely weather vanes to be blown about by any wind? Can they imagine that it satisfies to be physically available? A mistress shuts her door if the situation calls for it, or opens it because her heart is open.

The purist and the sensualist alike befoul sex by supposing it to be the purpose of itself—befoul in both senses: to besmirch, and to entangle and impede. On the one hand pleasure is damned as lust, while on the other it is upheld as a chief end, and both are a little bit right and terribly wrong. Both malign sex by making it a thing apart from other truths with which it shares a world.

No, I am not saying this well. Like all the others, I have said too much and too little. Like everyone else, you will have to define sex to yourself. Only remember that you alone can do it; it has a hundred million variations like fingerprints. Serve what you will, but in heaven's name, serve it; do not try to twist it to serve you.

Form and Reality

*M*atthew and I were outside the law and social custom, and to some extent outside our own beliefs, but we were not vicious. We did not grow horns or forked tongues, or become other than the personalities we started out with, only more concretely ourselves. That is one of the startling aspects of a love affair: it pitches one into the yes and no of reality, and you had not known you were not already there. Old forms won't serve; one is forced to search, and as the promise says, those who search quite often find. A love affair is highly educational, which is rarely emphasized. Matthew and I did a good deal of self-questioning in the beginning, usually in the privacy of our own minds, but a few times we compared notes.

Once he said, "What we are doing is wrong—"

"I know that," I said too quickly, having said it in the past.

"Yes," he agreed. "I was slower to accept it. But whatever the risks, I will bear them, because the alternative is not necessarily right. It can be a greater blunder to refuse a part of living."

That phrase, "a part of living," became for me a lens through which I saw our venture in perspective. Viewed in that way, it needed neither justification nor applause, but was merely itself.

We did not often speak these things aloud, not more than three of four times over the years. Since discussion and analysis can settle nothing in an extra-legal affair, it does no good and much harm to anatomize it. But that is equally true of married love. Discussion and analysis are almost always inferior to experience, except when they are a form of experience in themselves, in teaching for example.

Men are more apt to be romantic, I think, than women, partly because biologically they can afford to be. At all events, men invented romance, women did not, and it behooves us to speak low. Love is a kind of knowledge of another who is in one sense oneself. The knowledge is never total, but it is quite perfect in its sphere. It can be illogical, unreasonable, unmerited, inauspicious, and disorderly, and still retain that perfection, still be love. Take care how you rationalize it. Love is never debated into existence.

A spinster friend of mine wished devoutly to be married and, as often happens when events are warped out of their true time, she had exalted ideas of marital glories. In some desperation she accepted not the first man who asked her but more or less the last. It was a wholly unsuitable union, but she tried for seven years to make it into something it was not. After the inevitable breakup, she said to me with a kind of classic simplicity, "One thing I learned is that marriage is for amateurs."

That isn't all the truth, but it has a sting of discovery. She meant, of course, that all newcomers to marriage are inescapably beginners, a little clumsy, too earnest, quite unaware of what is yet required, cheerfully certain that they have arrived at a triumphant culmination instead of a precarious takeoff. A psychiatrist I know says it another way, that it takes gullibility to fall in love. That, too, is some of the truth.

Above all, amateurs are determined to make things go by rules. The amateur cook measures every drop and granule, frets if the pan is half an inch longer than the recipe calls for, relies zealously on the oven calibrator. The professional improvises materials and pans, and chops instead of shreds if it suits him, freely varies the oven heat if a hand stuck in tells him the temperature is wrong, and hang what the book says. Since my friend was not an amateur in other areas of her life—her work, friendships, education, diversions—she found it difficult to slow her intellect down to an emotional rate appropriate to a beginner.

The story is told of a woman who rushed up to the late Fritz Kreisler after a concert and cried, "Oh, Mr. Kreisler, I'd give my life to play as you do!" and the great violinist replied, "I did." The true professional gives everything, his very existence, and what he gets in return is nothing less than himself. He finds out who he is and what he is made of. There is no guarantee he will like who he is, but he will know something the amateur never learns. It is the old, old law that so exasperates amateurs: the only way to gain one's life—one's identity, one-self—is to lose it, to risk it. In that sense, a love affair is for professionals.

A married woman can get along nicely by ful-filling the outward forms of relationship, keeping up appearances, running a home well, savoring a social life. There is nothing wrong with that; those elements too are part of living and so much a part of marriage that it can stay afloat on them. But the wife who would not remain an amateur values these forms correctly, not mistaking them for love. A mistress does not have such forms to aid her; she has the inner reality or she has nothing. Like the professional artist, she is on her own, and if she does not like what she finds, at least she knows one kind of truth. All things are bought at a price; the relevant issues are the value of the article and whether one is going to haggle over paying.

It is time to say aloud that marriage is not so much the outcome of love, sex, or maturity as one road to them, even now the most available road for most people. Marriage is the logical next stage in human development. after childhood and youth, and the paradox is that developed powers clamor to be used. To marry is to invite growth, which induces more growth and demands a wider field. Love begets love, as the psychologists recognize, and they advocate ideally a loving home for all children as a means of nurturing and continuing the pattern. But they fail to follow their own insight through to the end: Marriage and the family are a natural extension of the initial human condition; in this context, whether marriage is happy or unhappy is not very important. The point is, it teaches; it completes one's growth, positively or negatively. And then what? Does one jump off a cliff, or else mark time for the rest of one's years? Does the choice lie between terminating the marriage and lapsing into a coma of expedience?

There is an alternative, but it is hard. Perhaps the deepest obligation of life is to put off what is outgrown, even when it was true in its day and has served us well, and to achieve as much reality as we are individually capable of. St. Paul said, "When I was a child, I spake as a child; I thought as a child, I understood as a child; but when I became a man, I put away childish things." To fail of that is to fail, period, and failure is the bitterest thing in life, because *it is unnecessary.* It lies with the individual to change it. The trouble is that we refuse the adult assignment of becoming selves and settle for becoming caricatures. When we can say, "I was wrong," "I make my own joy," "I find the world good," and not, "He mistreated me," "No one understands my needs," "They let me down," then we shall be adults, professionals with the capacity to love and be loved. The ultimate call upon every man and woman is to put away childish things, one of which is having conditions arranged for us.

When marriage has fulfilled its promise of rounding out personality, people frequently decide they have fallen out of love, or were never in it in the first place; or that marriage has proved a cheat;

or that one partner has betrayed the other. These charges may be valid or not. What really needs to be considered is that here one is, stuck with a self, and what shall be done with it from this point on, not how one arrived at it. Some men and some women find an answer in their work. Some engage in real or ersatz public service. Some venture into fleeting or lasting love affairs. Many, probably most, simply give up.

If all that glitters is not sex, all that breaks away from form is not morally reprehensible, either. It can be adult yearning to partake of an adult world, to create forms rather than to follow them; that is to say, to move from heteronomy to autonomy, which is what life is all about. It is possible for such full-scale development to occur within the framework of marriage, but not if the framework is substituted for the development itself. I am not a cartographer to map out the way for any given marriage; what is precisely needed is the willingness to do without maps, or rather to make one's own, to be inventive, to imagine and dare. Reality always lies beyond the loss of inherited forms, and between emerging from the latter and into the former is a trackless desert that frightens and dissuades many people from trying on themselves. To be afraid is sensible; this is dangerous territory. What is not so sensible is to fancy that shutting one's eyes shall have made the desert go away.

Love is the one creative force more or less accessible to everyone, the one chance offered to all to be an artist in his or her degree, whatever one's other talents may be. As any thinker or artist or mathematician knows, all creative endeavor has three fundamental conditions: (1) it arises from asymmetry or disorder; (2) it demands professionalism; (3) it imposes limits. In a love affair these conditions are more or less apparent from the outset, but a marriage has to construct them for itself, if it wishes to keep love an essential dweller in its house. One can build an entirely effective marriage without love, and that, too, must be recognized and accepted as a legitimate form. A love affair without love is a contradiction and cannot exist; it simply vanishes. A mistress has limited time, limited room, limited prerogatives, but she learns that limits are not a disadvantage. On the contrary, they are an indispensable element of creative design. A painting has an outer edge; music has structure and comes to a stop. So does life. To be a being is to have limits. We should be spongy and repulsive without the skin that marks where we leave off and the rest of the world begins. Minds and hearts need a skin, a limit, so that they shall not be vague and shapeless. In one sense marriage is its own antagonist: its very boundlessness and totality swamp its creative potential, unless one learns what creativity is and imposes its structured demands.

Matthew astonished me once by saying, "We've got to get the urgency out of this. We'll never really know what we have until we get the drama out of it."

I laughed at him. "Now you're doing the housework." He scowled, and I explained, "Look, we trust each other because we are trustworthy people, but each time we meet it is a new decision, and that's good. If there is time, we will acquire some habits, because people do, but when habit is all of it, without urgency or drama, I shall quit. Drama is only meaning, you know; it pulls a lot of diffused things into focus."

"Yes," he said, "I see. I like that."

It is difficult to write a good play, but it is still easier to write a play than to be one, which is what all of us are trying to do. There is profound reason in this. Man's impulse toward art, from the mute paleolithic cave paintings to Sophocles and Shakespeare, is bound up with a perception of our apartness from other creatures. Form and structure, selection and integration, are not playthings but necessities, and the one arena open to all is our own lives. One measure of a good play, of dramatic effectiveness, is change that is completed—not falsely tied up into a neat package, not by any means a happy ending, but a working through or resolution of those particular events into their meaning or reason.

The drama of a love affair is not mere entertainment and shadow play; it brings with it the possibility of moments of completeness, and the understanding that total and final solutions are as false in life as in literature.

In a high speed and loose age where the designs of good living are no more established, the whole problem of form and reality is sticky, personal, complicated, and saturates every level of existence. There is a school of thought among physicists and biologists that form is dead. One of these scientists told me that all one can see of another human being is dead and in the process of being sloughed off—the hair, the skin, the entire exterior covering. According to this school, life is a striving toward form, or perfection if you will, but the moment that is accomplished, it becomes static. To save itself, the principle or reality of life must destroy its forms and begin anew. This could explain even that which in our anguish and ignorance we mistake for an arch-foe: death itself. Death may be merely the total dissolution of form and reestablishment of the asymmetry necessary to perpetuate the creativity we know as life.

Habit is not by itself an evil. It often helps to mold the forces at play by providing channels in which they can gather themselves. That is why arranged marriages have worked down through the ages: they gave shape to many loose realities, including love. It was said: marry first, on rational grounds, and love may come afterward, and not infrequently, it did. But the assumption that the reality or force comes automatically with the adoption of form or is contained by it, is deadly.

Many years ago, when I was divorced initially against my choice, I protested to a friend, a much older man, "I was a good wife!" and he replied, "My dear, there is no such thing. There is only the right wife for a given man." That gave me pause, and a lopsided kind of comfort. It helped me to see that the pursuit of an abstract form—"a good wife"—is not the same thing as actual relationship arising from real forces. For the first time I realized that the causes of my broken marriage lay partly with me. But it took a long love affair to show me fully what my friend meant.

Society has rigid ideas of what constitutes a good wife, but a good mistress is one lone man's

business. An affair is free to make its own defini-
tions and rules—and make them it will, for human
beings do not live comfortably without a code;
even the underworld has a code, and a strict one.
But where, for example, a husband is almost compelled to be a good provider, and a wife to manage
his money well, if a mistress scatters his wealth on
the wind, that is his problem. Society may think
him a fool but it does not want to hear about it, and
that is very nice for the two people involved. The
financial arrangement between lovers begins and
ends with them; it is in no way obliged to adapt or
to be adapted to any other couple. This freedom
from compunction applies to almost everything
else—their sex lives, their faithfulness, their holi-
days, manners, diversions, duties, friends. Society
designates itself a third and far from silent partner
in a marriage; if it condemns or ignores a liaison, at
least it keeps its nose out. Thus a mistress is not
constrained to catechize herself with being a
"good" mistress, it is evident from the beginning
that there is no such thing. She is herself, and that
suffices or it does not.

Marriage radically needs more of this public-
be-damned attitude. A wife can too easily become
occupied with proving the system right, and fitting
herself into it, instead of giving her allegiance to the

hearts that live within the framework, her own and her husband's. In short, she bogs down in form and loses track of reality. Unpremeditated joy, a disregard of consequences, is one of the special ingredients of a love affair. Of course such spontaneity cannot be complete in a social world, but neither can consequences substitute for joy nor do consequences cause it. The joy of the moment, of uncalculatedness, is sadly missing from many lives and there is hunger for it, among men especially.

A man said to me, "I fell in love with my wife because she did not mind getting soaked in a rainstorm, and she had freckles on her nose, and she was mad for corn muffins. But she loved me because I was good to my mother and sister and paid my bills."

Anything goes if people make it go, and not otherwise. Marriage is not dialectics; men and women have loved well under the most impossible social systems, as dictators sometimes learn to their dismay. Love is, by its very nature, always in spite of systems, no matter how excellent, and not owing to them. One of the oldest delusions of man is that there must be, somewhere, a process that will guarantee love, or creative output, or salvation. It absolutely is not so, and over and over again we have to learn that experience is nearly always superior to formula or process or technique. There is that limb, and nobody can go out on it in one's stead. To go out on it is hazardous, but it is better than to hang oneself from it.

I implore you: trust your instincts. One pays a terrible price for a system or rule or authority that will always tell one what to do, and what is worse, what to think. The loss of insight is the blackest of all losses. In any decision in your marriage, the principal question is what *you* want. This sounds dissident to western ears, but it is nevertheless fundamental. All other questions—of children, money, home, position, families, work, friends, survival—while legitimate, are derivative; that is to say, without the marriage these questions would not exist, or they would take a very different form. The answers to them will be satisfactory and lasting only after the basic matter of personal wants is faced. If you cannot discern what it is you desire, you grope in a fog of dissatisfactions without really knowing why, and hit out in all the wrong directions. I do not suggest that a wife's own wishes are the sole consideration, nor that they are always right or always obtainable. I do argue that unless she can see what she wants and is willing to face it objectively, she is trying to get somewhere from nowhere. Wanting something is not wicked, it is human; and to renounce one's humanity with the expectation of being admired and cherished for it is at least illogical. Self-sacrifice can sometimes be an evasion of responsibility.

For a mistress this is an already cleared area. She does not have to chop out the underbrush of pre-accepted forms; she has already let go of forms. She never says to herself, What do other mistresses want? Or, What according to the rules ought I want? According to the rules, she ought not to exist, so the question is irrelevant. Rather, she examines truly what she does want. She may realize it is impossible, she may renounce it for base or noble reasons; she may lay claim to it and when the time comes pay the piper. But she decides from some degree of reality and not upon the forms that so readily become merely good form, manners, mores.

For all her infraction of the rules, a mistress is much more integrated into the larger designs of living than the average wife. She is not, like a wife, isolated, physically or mentally or emotionally, and thus cornered into defending her own importance. A mistress is often a very great friend, but she never tries to be a pal or substitute for men friends. It is simply not the same order of relationship, and she recognizes and defends the right of other orders to exist—partly because she has and needs others for herself. She is perhaps more like a man, in his human characteristics, than a wife is.

There are places where a woman—whether wife or mistress—does not belong, and this neither shatters her self-confidence nor offends her. She has her own areas of privacy where a man may not intrude. Like any human being, a mistress acquires part of her self-image from the impact she makes on others, but she is not wholly constituted of the impressions she makes. Thus, subterfuge is of no aid or attraction to her. She does not say things in hope of contradiction, such as "You don't love me," "That woman is prettier than I," "Don't buy me a birthday gift," hoping to be corrected.

I once said to Matthew, "I am a bad woman." I was mocking myself a little, but his rejoinder startled me.

"I know," he said. "It's delightful." I learned on the spot that a certain veracity of spirit and speech is essential to love's remaining love. Continual attempts to wring from a situation proof of its reality and worth, falsifies it. It ceases to be a relationship, a meeting, and becomes any of a hundred other things, a demand for reassurance, laziness, stubbornness, tyranny, all kinds of things. No one is so serene and so detached as never to need some approbation, but emotional blackmail does violence to love without really satisfying the other longing. Chicanery has never produced a shred of genuine response, which is what the heart wisely hungers for.

A mistress who likes and wants to hold her position does not presume a millimeter beyond a man's exact words, nor that what is said is not what is meant. A promise to come tomorrow if he can is not a sworn oath, and she keeps the distinction clear in her mind. Courts of law try cases fairly strictly on face value, admitting motives only where they can be shown by some tangible, visible evidence, or the courts would become hopelessly entangled in a web of supposition and there could be no ideal justice. So a love affair quickly falls of its own weight unless it proceeds on the presumption of a fair field. This affords it a refreshing reality that marriage could profit from adopting. Observing some marriages, I wonder whether wives want love or victory.

I have been young and now am old; I have been wife, mother, and mistress. From my mountain peak of years, I can only conclude that many people do not want love, and they use marriage as a bulwark against it, however unlikely that may sound. Oh yes, they make all the appropriate noises, but they don't really want to be disturbed. In some half-buried memory, they know that strong emotion extracts a price it frightens them to think of paying out of their meager resources—a price of effort, courage, attention. They would rather read about great loves or watch them on a screen than participate in them.

Only the picayune personality is terrified of being overwhelmed, while the larger spirit longs for it. The paltry soul fears that its ramshackle building will be blown away in the storms of living; the bold nature shouts in the teeth of the gale, glad to be hammered into shape and purpose, that it may discover what it is made of. The cautious hedge themselves about with customs and plans and prefabricated diversions, and appeal to experts to certify that what they do is genuine living. But life is a deeper process, filled with the highly charged winds of paradox and truth and transfiguration, a willingness for tears, a sense of ending. Don't pretend you want love if what you truly want is safety, like the kitten who stalks its mother's tail, knowing it will get cuffed, and then washed and warmed and fed.

It is not a young wife's fault is she confuses mental and physical housekeeping with love. She is so constantly admonished that the success or

118

failure of her marriage is almost entirely her job. It is distinctly not a mistress's job. The state of her union receives her alert attention, but not exclusively, and her job is, as it always was, identity. If a man wishes communication with that identity to continue, he too must make contribution toward that end. In Dante's poem, the couple wholly engrossed by love both ended up in hell, not the man alone. Love turned wholly back upon itself, seeking to sustain itself on its own nature with no input from the world, is headed for schizophrenia, a destruction of personality, woman's as well as man's.

A mistress needs intelligence and cultivates it. So does a wife, and she should stop her ears to those who urge her not to cultivate it. Not because enthusiasm wanes and people grow old, and not because "love is not enough," the catch phrase of the past that we thought so marvelously enlightened. Love is quite enough if it is indeed love and not some too-young and uncomprehending prototype, which of course it has to be in the beginning. How else is one to learn? Nor is intelligence a last resort to "hold" a husband, like an ingenious toy to divert a child. If he needs holding, let go. What follows will at least be interesting, and interest is better than boredom any day—unless of course what one really wants is not to be troubled, and

119

then it is petulant to complain of having had one's wish granted.

Intellectual bankruptcy is no more attractive than any other kind of poverty. Intelligence is necessary for oneself first, and after that for love to come alive in. Any man who is drawn solely to surfaces and youthful charm is eventually not going to be enough of a man for the woman you shall have become, if you grow at all. It is just that simple. Love is vastly more than sex and family life, a social unit, an economic cog, no matter how superbly marriage fills these niches. Love is a wealth of community where mind, body, and spirit meet and dissolve, to gather again in new dimensions and forms. It is as matter-of-fact as two plus two, and as far-reaching and complex as the galaxy.

If I have made Matthew sound superior to other men, that is not because he was so, but because I loved him. Love is not concerned with comparisons, to prove one person better than another, nor is it blind. On the contrary, it is clearest perception, and what it perceives is that the living human being is unique and wonderful. All the everyday processes of seeing, hearing, walking, thinking, speaking, waking, are seen to be lovely, and this loveliness is at the same time their inner reality. To love is to see that there is worth in living, and those who love find in themselves a corresponding worth that cannot be repudiated.

It is useful and possibly important to note that the title *Mrs.* is a contraction from *Mistress*. Both terms are historically civil salutations. Even the word *wife* was so used. It was once correct to address a decent woman as "wife" or "goodwife," implying a certain dignity, as the French confer "madame" upon all women over a certain age, regardless of their marital status. The Bible speaks of "a married wife," as if there would be unmarried wives, which indeed there have been throughout the centuries as the canny old prophets knew.

In Elizabethan times a mistress was either a married woman or one who had earned community position as a tavern-keeper or baker or midwife. A mistress meant female master, a woman who had command of something—a household, a farm, a shop, a craft. It is revealing and disquieting that wives have let the term *mistress* go by default to women who wield but one kind of power—at least, as wives imagine. In point of fact, they wield many more.

A woman who loves outside the law cannot survive as an amateur. She must acquire mastery over many arts, and she yields only when and to whom she will. When she surrenders, it is an act of will, not a ritual. No person living has ever attained complete mastery over the self, but a mistress is bound to try and given scope to do it in. "She considereth a field and buyeth it, and planteth a vineyard: she seeketh wool, and flax, and worketh willingly with her hands: she perceiveth that her merchandise is good: her candle goeth not out by night; she is not afraid of snow, for all her household are clothed in scarlet; she stretcheth out her hand to the poor; she openeth her mouth with wisdom, and in her tongue is the law of kindness." This is her goal and criterion.

A married woman whom I have known a long time, though not intimately, once alluded obliquely to my status as a mistress. She said recently, on a rainy afternoon, "Whenever I have encountered you over the years, I have thought, 'There with the grace of God go I.' " It was an extraordinary thing for a wife to say. Could I have said it to someone like me if I had been a legal wife instead of what I was? I don't know. A look passed between us as women, and I knew that wives and mistresses, if they learn anything at all, learn pretty much the same things. We take different roads but we arrive at the same destination. Her geniality and greatness of heart are one reason I have written this all down. When one is young, and a new wife, it is easy to forget that the first and last requirement is to be woman.

Matthew is dead. What remains is the light and shadow of having lived.